The Journey of Columbus

Written by Melinda Lilly
Illustrated by Raquel Díaz

Educational Consultants

Kimberly Weiner, Ed.D
Betty Carter, Ed.D

Rourke
Publishing LLC
Vero Beach, Florida 32963

www.rourkepublishing.com

A mis amigos de Versal, marineros de este nuevo viaje.
To my friends at Versal, crewmates on this new voyage.
—R. D.

Designer: Elizabeth J. Bender

Art Direction: Rigo Aguirre, www.versalgroup.com

Library of Congress Cataloging-in-Publication Data

Lilly, Melinda.
    The journey of Columbus / Melinda Lilly; illustrated by Raquel Díaz.
        p. cm. — (Reading American history)
    Summary: Briefly presents Christopher Columbus's 1492 journey from Spain into the unknown.
    ISBN 1-58952-358-X (hardcover)
    1. Columbus, Christopher—Juvenile literature. 2. Columbus, Christopher—Journeys—Juvenile literature. 3. Explorers—America—Biography—Juvenile literature. 4. Explorers—Spain—Biography—Juvenile literature. 5. America—Discovery and exploration—Spanish—Juvenile literature. [1. Columbus, Christopher. 2. Explorers. 3. America—Discovery and exploration—Spanish.] I. Díaz, illus. II. Title.

E111 .L7675 2003
970.01'5—dc21   2002001038

Cover Illustration: Columbus and the Niña, Pinta, and Santa Maria

Printed in the USA

Time Line

Help students follow this story by introducing important events in the Time Line.

100   The compass is invented in China.

1492   Columbus reaches the Americas.

1498   Vasco da Gama arrives in India by way of the Cape of Good Hope.

1506   Columbus dies.

1513   Juan Ponce de León lands in Florida.

1522   Magellan's ship and 18 crew members complete circumnavigation of world.

1609   Henry Hudson explores the New York area.

Columbus sets off for **Asia.**

The ships sail in 1492.

Columbus at sea

Weeks pass on the ships **Niña**, **Pinta**, and **Santa Maria**.

The ships

"Go back!" the **sailors** say.

The sailors and Columbus

The sailors think the **world** is flat. The sailors do not want to fall off the flat world.

Sailors look at the map.

Columbus knows the world is not flat.

Columbus with his map

Columbus sails on.

On the **journey**

"Land! Land!" yells a sailor.

A sailor spots land.

Columbus is not in Asia.

The ships stop at an **island** in the **Americas**.

The ships come to the Americas.

Soon, many more people will know of the Americas.

Columbus comes back home.

Word List

Americas (uh MER ih kuz)—The American continents

Asia (AY zhuh)—A continent that is next to Europe and the Pacific, Arctic, and Indian oceans

Columbus, Christopher (Kuh LUM bus, KRIS tuh fer)—An important explorer, Christopher Columbus sailed to islands in the Caribbean in 1492.

island (EYE lund)—Land that is surrounded by water and is too small to be a continent

journey (JUR nee)—A trip

Niña (NEEN yuh)—One of Columbus's ships

Pinta (PEEN tuh)—One of Columbus's ships

sailors (SAY lurz)—People who work on a ship

Santa Maria (SAN tuh muh REE uh) The flagship of Columbus's 1492 journey

world (WURLD)—The globe, the Earth

Books to Read

Dekay, James. *Meet Christopher Columbus*. Random House, 2001.

Devillier, Christy. *Christopher Columbus*. Abdo & Daughters, 2002.

Fontanez, Edwin. *Taino: The Activity Book*. Exit Studio, 1996.

Roop, Peter and Connie Roop. *Christopher Columbus*. Scholastic, 2001.

Websites to Visit

www.ibiblio.org/expo/1492.exhibit/Intro.html

www1.minn.net/%7Ekeithp/

www.childfun.com/themes/columbus.shtml

www.fordham.edu/halsall/source/columbus1.html

http://search.biography.com/print_record.pl?id=4596

Index